NARADA BHAKTI SUTRA

Essence and Sanskrit Grammar

Ashwini was born in Ludhiana in his mother's home and completed his pre-University from Govt. College for Boys. He has also written texts on Sanskrit Grammar delving into Panini's Ashtadhyayi.

From the same Author:

Bhagavad Gita for Chanting
Bhagavad Gita Reader: All Verses in 4 Quarters
Bhagavad Gita Recitation — pocket book
Bhagavad Gita Dhyana Yoga: Commentary and Grammar – 6th Chapter
Bhagavad Gita: Yoga of Self Control — 6th Chapter
Bhagavad Gita Applied Wisdom
Bhagavad Gita Heart and Soul

The Sanskrit Alphabet
Conversations with Space
Maya the Golden Veil
Tao Te Ching Brahman
Ishavasya Upanishad: Essence and Sanskrit Grammar

Ashtadhyayi of Panini Complete
Maheshwar Sutras Pratyaharas
Dhatupatha Handbook
Dhatupatha Sutras Enumerated
Dhatupatha Verbs in 5 Lakaras — in three volumes
Dhatupatha of Panini: Accented Roots with English Meanings
and Verbs iii/1 forms in Present Tense

Rudra Puja: Simple Complete Profound
Rudra Puja Mantras — pocket book

Patanjali Yoga Sutras: Essence and Sanskrit Grammar
Patanjali Yoga Sutras Essence
Magic Sutras Potent — pocket book

ॐ

NARADA BHAKTI

SUTRA

Essence and Sanskrit Grammar

Ashwini Kumar Aggarwal

जय गुरुदेव

© 2019, Ashwini Kumar Aggarwal
ISBN10:   93-5351-151-8
ISBN13: 978-93-5351-151-7
Paperback Edition

Title: Narada Bhakti Sutra
SubTitle: Essence and Sanskrit Grammar

Printed and Published by Ashwini Kumar Aggarwal
The Art of Living Centre
147 Punjabi Bagh, Patiala 147001
Punjab, India

https://advaita56.weebly.com/
Devotees of Sri Sri Ravi Shankar Ashram

https://www.artofliving.org/

10th February 2019, Basant Panchami, Uttarayana
Saraswati Puja, Onset of Spring, Dress code Yellow
Revati Nakshatra, Shukla Paksha, Magha Masa
Vikram Samvat 2075 Virodhakrit, Saka Era 1940 Vilambi

1st Edition February 2019

जय गुरुदेव

Dedication

Sri Sri Ravi Shankar

who has lit the flame in our hearts

Blessing

Life springs from love – the origin is love and life seeks love… Having attained that, human life becomes perfect. Love brings such fulfillment in life.

Sri Sri Ravi Shankar
Narada Bhakti Sutra – A Bridge to the Divine

Preface

Our epics the Ramayana and Mahabharata, and our puranas the Srimad Bhagavatam and Devi Bhagavatam recount wondrous events of courage, devotion, duty and selfless service. They have enriched our planet immeasurably. Even today quite a good number of persons and organizations epitomize that exemplary valor, steadfastness and cheerfulness.

Bhakti is a very special attitude. It is a rare kind of lifestyle. It requires tremendous guts, large-heartedness and purity of vision. Narada was an adventurer from long ago, who exemplified the qualities of a Bhakta.

We have heard the famous quote – Beauty lies in the eyes of the Beholder. This is what Narada lived. To him each and every one was divine, so he extended his hand to the cruelest sinner and to the most benevolent king. He went out of his way to have a dialogue with serpents and goblins - braving harsh mountains and rough weathers - demons and despots, commoners, officers, soldiers, saints and children.

Narada exuded such warmth and caring, he brought such innocence and spontaneity in his wake, that he not only infused his surroundings with vitality, but also imparted a measure of grace.

This is the story of the values he lived, that an ancient sage penned down. It has come down to us as priceless nuggets evoking awe and inspiration. It has the charm of taking us on a journey to freedom.

For the students of Sanskrit grammar, copious notes giving the case of each word have been clearly listed. Even today someone asks me, why Sanskrit?

Listen to the Sound of the Veena and you may know. Listen to a Vedic Chant or a Bhajan and something opens up. The manner in which the Sanskrit words and phrases have been constructed does something to the anatomy. Narada is credited with inventing the Veena, a lyre or lute musical instrument, which he is said to play often. The soothing strains grab our attention well before his arrival. The 24 frets in a Veena mirror the 24 separate vertebrae in the spine, and its 7 strings mirror the 7 chakras. Even the varied inflections and subtlety of a human voice can be distinctly heard in a Veena concert.

This is the aim of Bhakti, to light the flame of love in every heart, to make the bud blossom.

Suffice to say that drinking the nectar from the satsang of a Living Master, attending a live concert is the way to experience the bliss of Bhakti.

Contents

Latin Transliteration

International Alphabet of Sanskrit Transliteration (I.A.S.T.)

a	ā	i	ī	u	ū	ṛ	ṝ	ḷ	
अ	आ	इ	ई	उ	ऊ	ऋ	ॠ	ऌ	
						ॢ	ॣ	ॢ	
e	ai	o	au	ṃ	m̐	ḥ	Ardha Visarga	oṃ	
ए	ऐ	ओ	औ	◌ं	◌ँ	◌:	ᳵ	ॐ	

Consonants are shown with a vowel 'a= अ' for uttering									
ka	क	ca	च	ṭa	ट	ta	त	pa	प
kha	ख	cha	छ	ṭha	ठ	tha	थ	pha	फ
ga	ग	ja	ज	ḍa	ड	da	द	ba	ब
gha	घ	jha	झ	ḍha	ढ	dha	ध	bha	भ
ṅa	ङ	ña	ञ	ṇa	ण	na	न	ma	म
ya	ra	la	va		ḷa	'			
य	र	ल	व		ळ	ऽ			
				Consonant only					
śa	ṣa	sa	ha		ka	क्अ = क			
श	ष	स	ह		k	क्			

Prayer

ॐ नमो भगवते वासुदेवाय

ॐ नमो भगवते वासुदेवाय

ॐ नमो भगवते वासुदेवाय

ॐ नमो भगवते वासुदेवाय

oṃ namo bhagavate vāsudevāya
oṃ namo bhagavate vāsudevāya
oṃ namo bhagavate vāsudevāya
oṃ namo bhagavate vāsudevāya

अथातो भक्ति व्याख्यास्यामः ॥ १

athāto bhaktiṃ vyākhyāsyāmaḥ ॥ 1

अथ अतः भक्तिम् व्याख्या-स्यामः ॥ १
Now therefore Bhakti elucidate-shall.

अथ ^{0} अतः ^{0}
(वयम् $^{mfn1/3}$)   भक्तिम् $^{f2/1}$ व्याख्या-स्यामः लृट् $^{iii/3}$ ॥
Now therefore we shall elucidate Bhakti.

भक्ति from Dhatupatha root - 998 भज सेवायाम् । In Paninian Grammar it declines as a feminine stem.

अथ = now   अतः = therefore
Adverbs in Sanskrit are indeclinable generally.

व्याख्या-स्यामः = It is a common practice in Sanskrit grammar to use a "hyphen" to indicate compounds.

Compound or समास is frequently encountered in Sanskrit literature. It has a beauty and a brevity.

Theme 1 Beginning

1. When a sage speaks, it carries weight. The start is profound. Simple. Direct. Short. To the point.

सा त्वस्मिन् परमप्रेमरूपा ॥ २

sā tvasmin paramapremarūpā ॥ 2

सा तु अस्मिन् परम–प्रेम–रूपा ॥ २

अस्मिन् [n7/1] तु [0] सा [f1/1] परम–प्रेम–रूपा [f1/1] (भवति [ऌड् iii/1]) ॥

Intrinsically in this state it is the highest , purest love.

पोथी पढ़ पढ़ जग मुआ, पंडित भया न कोय ।

ढ़ाई आखर प्रेम का, पढ़ै सो पंडित होय ॥

Kabir, circa 1500 CE

Payoji Maine Ram Ratan Dhan Payo-Lata Mangeshkar
https://www.youtube.com/watch?v=sUqA69N_0MM

Mirabai, 1498-1546 CE

Namami Shamishan Nirvan Roopam - Various
https://www.youtube.com/watch?v=0eF5El54DZM

Tulsidas, ? -1623 CE

Hanuman Chalisa - Hariharan
https://www.youtube.com/watch?v=AETFvQonfV8

Tulsidas, ? -1623 CE

Japji Sahib english rendering – Sarvjit Singh
https://oboroi.com/

Guru Nanak, 1469-1539 CE

Theme 2 Definition

2. Life is in a state of constant flux. It varies moment to moment. A new thought springs up, some emotion comes, plans are continuously made and remade.

Bhakti is the state of Love. Love is what we are made up of. But at any given time, love has changed into something else. That something else is exciting or depressing. It is attracting or repelling. Or just plain boring. When the divine moment resurfaces, when the flame inside shines bright, that is Bhakti.

अमृतस्वरूपा च ॥ ३

amṛtasvarūpā ca ॥ 3

अमृत–स्वरूपा च ॥ ३

अमृत–स्वरूपा $^{f1/1}$ च^{0} ॥

And it has the effect of nectar.

Theme 3 The Nectar

3. Nectar is rare. Just a drop of nectar goes a long way. It develops some startling superhuman energy that lasts and powers our days, fulfills our aspirations.

Bhakti is that nectar. It has that intrinsic quality. Divine Love has that power.

यल्लब्ध्वा पुमान् सिद्धो भवति अमृतो भवति तृप्तो भवति ॥ ४

yallabdhvā pumān siddho bhavati amṛto bhavati
tṛpto bhavati ॥ 4

यत् लब्ध्वा पुमान् सिद्धः भवति अमृतः भवति तृप्तः भवति ॥ ४

यत् $^{n1/1}$ लब्ध्वा $^{क्त्वा\ 0}$ पुमान् $^{m1/1}$ सिद्धः $^{m1/1}$ भवति $^{लट्\ iii/1}$
अमृतः $^{m1/1}$ भवति $^{लट्\ iii/1}$ तृप्तः $^{m1/1}$ भवति $^{लट्\ iii/1}$ ॥

क्त्वा = Indeclinable past participle, gerund. Used in
the sense of "having done", for a *root without an
upasarga.*

यत् लब्ध्वा -> यल्लब्धवा । Consonant Sandhi 8.4.60 तोर्लि ।
सिद्धः भवति -> सिद्धो भवति । Visarga Sandhi
6.1.114 हशि च । and then 6.1.87 आद् गुणः ।

Theme 4 Liberation

4. One who drinks the nectar of Bhakti becomes perfected. He is satiated. He attains liberation.

यत्प्राप्य न किंचिद्वाञ्छति न शोचति न द्वेष्टि न रमते नोत्साही भवति ॥ ५

yatprāpya na kiṃcidvāñchati na śocati na dveṣṭi na ramate notsāhī bhavati ॥ 5

यत् प्राप्य न किंचित् वाञ्छति न शोचति न द्वेष्टि न रमते न उत्साही भवति ॥ ५

यत् $^{n1/1}$ प्राप्य $^{ल्यप्\ 0}$ न ^{0} किंचित् ^{0} वाञ्छति $^{लट्\ iii/1}$ न ^{0} शोचति $^{लट्\ iii/1}$ न ^{0} द्वेष्टि $^{लट्\ iii/1}$ न ^{0} रमते $^{लट्\ iii/1}$ न ^{0} उत्साही $^{m1/1}$ भवति $^{लट्\ iii/1}$ ॥

ल्यप् = Indeclinable past participle, *gerund*. Used in the sense of "having done", for a *root prefixed with an upasarga*.

उत्साहिन् = stem that is an adjective, i.e. can decline in any gender as per context.

Theme 5 Sorrow Enmity Evaporated

5. One who drinks the nectar of Bhakti has no more craving. His sorrows are wiped out. Enmity has left him. Entertainment no longer prods him, nor does any distraction worry him.

यज्ज्ञात्वा मत्तो भवति स्तब्धो भवति आत्मारामो भवति ॥ ६

yajjñātvā matto bhavati, stabdho bhavati,

ātmārāmo bhavati ॥ 6

यत् ज्ञात्वा मत्तः भवति स्तब्धः भवति आत्म-आरामः भवति ॥ ६

यत् $^{n1/1}$ ज्ञात्वा $^{क्त्वा\,0}$

(सः $^{m1/1}$)   मत्तः $^{क\,m1/1}$ भवति $^{लट्\,iii/1}$

स्तब्धः $^{क\,m1/1}$ भवति $^{लट्\,iii/1}$

आत्म-आरामः $^{m1/1}$ भवति $^{लट्\,iii/1}$ ॥

क = past participle passive. Used in the sense of past

tense.

Theme 6 Dawn of Peace

6. Which having experienced, he gets intoxicated. He gets wonderstruck.

He enjoys himSelf, the peace dawns in him.

सा न कामयमाना निरोधरूपत्वात् ॥ ७

sā na kāmayamānā nirodharūpatvāt ॥ 7

सा न कामयमाना निरोध–रूपत्वात् ॥ ७

सा $^{f1/1}$ न ^{0} कामयमाना $^{f1/1}$

निरोध–रूपत्वात् $^{n5/1}$ ॥

सा = a feminine pronoun is used to indicate भक्ति Bhakti, that declines like a feminine.

Theme 7 Lust Quenched

7. That Bhakti doesn't have an iota of lust or fickle desire.

Because it stems from pacifism. It is a **renunciation** of all that is disturbing, transient or worthless.

निरोधस्तु लोकवेदव्यापारन्यासः ॥ ८

nirodhastu lokavedavyāpāranyāsaḥ ॥ 8

निरोधः तु लोक–वेद–व्यापार–न्यासः ॥ ८
निरोधः $^{m1/1}$ तु ^{0} लोक–वेद–व्यापार–न्यासः $^{m1/1}$ ॥

Many times a Sanskrit sentence is without the verb भवति that means "is". It is implicitly understood for brevity and beauty in chanting.

Theme 8 Wisdom of Bhakti

8. Indeed a JUDICIOUS application of renouncing worldly entanglements, onerous religious rituals, and frivolous materialistic transactions.

तस्मिन्ननन्यता तद्विरोधिषूदासीनता च ॥ ९

tasminnananyatā tadvirodhiṣūdāsīnatā ca ॥ 9

तस्मिन् अनन्यता तद्-विरोधिषु उदासीनता च ॥ ९

तस्मिन् $^{m7/1}$ अनन्यता $^{f1/1}$

तद्-विरोधिषु $^{m7/3}$ उदासीनता $^{f1/1}$ च ^{0} ॥

तद् = दकारान्तः पुंलिङ्गः 'तद्' शब्दः । During compound formation, the प्रातिपदिक stems are used and only the last stem gets the appropriate case ending.

Theme 9 No Defense Needed

9. In Bhakti there is a strong identity, a complete unity of the mind-body-soul.

And there is an indifference to ANYTHING that comes in the way. There is no defense, no resistance needed in Bhakti.

अन्याश्रयाणां त्यागोऽनन्यता ॥ १०

anyāśrayāṇāṃ tyāgo'nanyatā ॥ 10

अन्य–आश्रयाणाम् त्यागः अनन्यता ॥ १०

अन्य–आश्रयाणाम् $^{m6/3}$ त्यागः $^{m1/1}$ अनन्यता $^{f1/1}$ ॥

Theme 10 Strong Identity

10. A strong identity is being fully established in own self-respect and self-confidence. It means there is no need for external props or supports.

A Bhakta is so centered that nothing shakes his self-esteem, nor does he go about begging or bragging.

लोकवेदेषु तदनुकूलाचरणं तद्विरोधिषूदासीनता ॥ ११

lokavedeṣu tadanukūlācaraṇaṃ

tadvirodhiṣūdāsīnatā ॥ 11

लोक-वेदेषु तद्-अनुकूल-आचरणम् तद्-विरोधिषु उदासीनता ॥ ११

लोक-वेदेषु $^{m7/3}$ तद्-अनुकूल-आचरणम् $^{n2/1}$ तद्-विरोधिषु $^{m7/3}$

उदासीनता $^{f1/1}$ ॥

Theme 11 True Indifference

11. Practice being intensely engrossed in what you do, thus automatically you are **shielded** or indifferent to all who are not aligned to your lifestyle, or to anyone who is far removed from devotion.

भवतु निश्चयदार्ढ्यादूर्ध्वं शास्त्ररक्षणम् ॥ १२

bhavatu niścayadārḍhyādūrdhvaṃ
śāstrarakṣaṇam ॥ 12

भवतु निश्चय–दार्ढ्यात् ऊर्ध्वम् शास्त्र–रक्षणम् ॥ १२

निश्चय–दार्ढ्यात् $^{m5/1}$ ऊर्ध्वम् ^{0}

शास्त्र–रक्षणम् $^{n1/1}$ भवतु $^{लोट् \ iii/1}$ ॥

ऊर्ध्वम् = After.

Adverbs in Sanskrit are indeclinable generally.

Kumbh Mela – Prayagraj, Haridwar, Ujjain, Nasik
https://en.wikipedia.org/wiki/Kumbh_Mela

Navratri – The Art of Living Bangalore Ashram
https://www.artofliving.org/navratri

Theme 12 Culture Scripture Tradition

12. May you be firmly committed to guard and keep alive the culture, scripture and tradition of the community, even **after** having attained Liberation.

A bhakta or an enlightened saint has this quality ingrained in him. Even though he has reached the goal, he doesn't go slack in his daily efforts.

This verse is an implied Blessing as well to the one who has newly attained Freedom.

अन्यथा पातित्यशङ्कया ॥ १३

anyathā pātityaśaṅkayā ॥ 13

अन्यथा पातित्य–शङ्कया ॥ १३

अन्यथा [0]   पातित्य–शङ्कया [f3/1]   ॥

Theme 13 Negate the Risk

13. Or else there is the **risk** of falling down again.

Respect for and observance of age old traditions of the community you live in and their wise sayings is highly recommended.

लोकोऽपि तावदेव भोजनादिव्यापारस्त्वाशरीरधारणावधि ॥ १४

loko'pi tāvadeva

bhojanādivyāpārastvāśarīradhāraṇāvadhi ॥ 14

लोकः अपि तावत् एव भोजन–आदि–व्यापारः तु आ–शरीर–धारण–
अवधि ॥ १४

लोकः $^{m1/1}$ अपि ^{0} तावत् ^{0} एव ^{0}

भोजन-आदि-व्यापारः $^{m1/1}$ तु ^{0} आ-शरीर-धारण-अवधि ^{0} ॥

Theme 14 Social norms Body conduct

14. Indeed one must observe the social norms and protocols also.

And one must continue to maintain a discipline in food habits, exercise, sleep, etc. until we depart from this world by dropping the body.

तल्लक्षणानि वाच्यन्ते नानामतभेदात् ॥ १५

tallakṣaṇāni vācyante nānāmatabhedāt ॥ 15

तत्-लक्षणानि वाच्यन्ते नाना मत–भेदात् ॥ १५

नाना ^{0} मत–भेदात् $^{m5/1}$

तत्-लक्षणानि $^{n1/3}$ वाच्यन्ते $^{लट् कर्म॰ iii/3}$ ॥

वाच्यन्ते = लट् कर्मणि = Present Tense Passive voice

Theme 15 Expressions of Devotion

15. Many and diverse are the flavours of Bhakti.

These diverse expressions are being stated.

पूजादिष्वनुराग इति पाराशर्यः ॥ १६

pūjādiṣvanurāga iti pārāśaryaḥ ॥ 16

पूजा–आदिषु अनुरागः इति पाराशर्यः ॥ १६

पूजा–आदिषु m7/3   अनुरागः m1/1   इति 0   पाराशर्यः m1/1 ॥

Rudra Puja by Gurudev Sri Sri Ravi Shankar

https://www.artofliving.org/in-en/what-rudra-puja

https://www.youtube.com/watch?v=FojLU658tMI

Ancient Vedic Chants - Shangu Chakra Gadha Padmam

https://www.youtube.com/watch?v=zjcVbd1O7KQ&t

The Bhagavad Gita recited by Kumari Vanisree and

Kumari Vijayalakshmi of Ramakrishna Math, Bangalore

https://www.youtube.com/watch?v=vjIdTlkJJkA

Theme 16 Rudra Puja

16. According to sage Parashar, Bhakti is being steadfast in doing prayers and innately observing religious guidelines.

Immersing in beautiful worship like Rudra Puja is Bhakti.

कथादिष्विति गर्गः ॥ १७

kathādiṣviti gargaḥ ॥ 17

कथा–आदिषु इति गर्गः ॥ १७

कथा–आदिषु $^{m7/3}$ (अनुरागः $^{m1/1}$) इति ^{0} गर्गः $^{m1/1}$ ॥

अनुरागः = deep commitment. *Explicit in verse 16 and then implicit in some of the following verses.*

This is a classic usage of अनुवृत्ति Anuvritt i in Sanskrit literature. A principle or idea once stated is **reused** in the following sentences implicitly, i.e. it has a domain.

It is one of the founding principles of good software code, so computer science folks know all about it.

Theme 17 Srimad Bhagavat Katha

17. The sage Garg describes Bhakti as conducting spiritual discourses, relating stories of the Divine and organizing and participating in festivals and community celebrations.

Attending and being part of Satsang is Bhakti.

आत्मरत्यविरोधेनेति शाण्डिल्यः ॥ १८

ātmaratyavirodheneti śāṇḍilyaḥ ॥ 18

आत्म-रति-अविरोधेन इति शाण्डिल्यः ॥ १८

आत्म-रति-अविरोधेन $^{m3/1}$ इति ^{0} शाण्डिल्यः $^{m1/1}$ ॥

Theme 18 Rejoice in Self sans Conflict

18. Rishi Shandilya opines that Bhakti is delighting in the Self without any inhibition or prejudice.

Rejoice in the Self without Conflict, that is Bhakti.

नारदस्तु तदर्पिताखिलाचारता तद्विस्मरणे परमव्याकुलतेति ॥ १९

nāradastu tadarpitākhilācāratā tadvismaraṇe
paramavyākulateti ॥ 19

नारदः तु तद्-अर्पित–अखिल–आचारता तद्-विस्मरणे परम–
व्याकुलता इति ॥ १९

नारदः ^{m1/1}   तु ^0   तद्-अर्पित–अखिल–आचारता ^{f1/1}
तद्-विस्मरणे ^{m7/1}   परम–व्याकुलता ^{f1/1}   इति ^0   ॥

Theme 19 Offer yourself Completely

19. Narada says that offering each and every thought, word and deed at the feet of the Divine is the Devotion.

And experiencing sharp pangs of separation in every case of disconnection from the source, or whenever one has to do an activity that takes us away from the Divine, that is the mark of a devoted heart.

Forgetting to honour the Divine, forgetting to acknowledge the Divine presence, such when remembered becomes unbearable for the Bhakta.

अस्त्येवमेवम् ॥ २०

astyevamevam ॥ 20

अस्ति एवम् एवम् ॥ २०

अस्ति ^{लट् iii/1}　एवम्⁰　एवम्⁰ ॥

Theme 20 Bhakti has Infinite modes

20. For sure, such and many more likewise expressions of Bhakti exist.

As individuals we have our instincts, intuition, insight and temperament. Any pure expression, any word or act that enriches society, that touches hearts, that forges good-will, it is Bhakti.

Sages and Saints, Gurus and Masters, Noble men and women have lived many a divine life. Their words, habits and lifestyle might have been different; but there has been something deeply sacred, pure and respectful about them. Consider our ten Sikh Gurus.

यथा व्रजगोपिकानाम् ॥ २१

yathā vrajagopikānām ॥ 21

यथा व्रज–गोपिकानाम् ॥ २१
यथा [0]   व्रज–गोपिकानाम् [f6/3] ॥

Theme 21 Gopis of Krishna

21. O ! What scintillating devotion expressed by the gopis of Vrindavan.

The gopis had the remarkable attitude –
Come what may, I wish you to be happy. Do what thy will, my happiness is simply in thine happiness.

तत्रापि न माहात्म्यज्ञानविस्मृत्यपवादः ॥ २२

tatrāpi na māhātmyajñānavismṛtyapavādaḥ ॥ 22

तत्र अपि न माहात्म्य–ज्ञान–विस्मृति–अपवादः ॥ २२

तत्र [0] अपि [0] न [0] माहात्म्य–ज्ञान–विस्मृति–अपवादः [m1/1] ॥

Theme 22 Remember the Greatness

22. Also in the devotion of the **gopis**, there is not the slightest taint of forgetting the magnanimity of the Noble, the Great, the Sacred, the Wisdom.

तद्विहीनं जाराणामिव ॥ २३

tadvihīnaṃ jārāṇāmiva ॥ 23

तद्-विहीनम् जाराणाम् इव ॥ २३

तद्-विहीनम् [f1/1]   जाराणाम् [f6/3]   इव [0] ॥

Theme 23 Real Love

23. Certainly the love or attraction or excitement that is not based on **inner beauty**, on character, on strength, or honesty is simply a rotten kind of relationship.

नास्त्येव तस्मिंस्तत्सुखसुखित्वम् ॥ २४

nāstyeva tasmiṃstatsukhasukhitvam ॥ 24

नास्ति एव तस्मिन् तद्–सुख–सुखित्वम् ॥ २४

तस्मिन् $^{m7/1}$ एव ^{0} तद्–सुख–सुखित्वम् $^{तुमुन्\ 0}$ नास्ति $^{लट्\ iii/1}$ ॥

तुमुन् = Indeclinable Verb. Used in the sense of "to do", "to wish" or "to intend".

तस्मिन् तत् -> तस्मिंस्तत् । न् -> ंस्
Consonant Sandhi 8.3.7 नश्छव्यप्रशान् ।

तद्सुखसुखित्वम् -> तत्सुखसुखित्वम् । द् -> त्
Consonant Sandhi 8.4.55 खरि च ।

Theme 24 Casual Attraction

24. No such healthy relationship exists between casual lovers or in the excitement during dating.

सा तु कर्मज्ञानयोगेभ्योऽप्यधिकतरा ॥ २५

sā tu karmajñānayogebhyo'pyadhikatarā ॥ 25

सा तु कर्म–ज्ञान–योगेभ्यः अपि अधिकतरा ॥ २५

सा $^{f1/1}$ तु ^{0} कर्म–ज्ञान–योगेभ्यः $^{m5/3}$ अपि ^{0}

अधिकतरा $^{f1/1}$ ॥

Theme 25 Bhakti = Karma Jnana Yoga

25. Indeed such Bhakti matches the attainment of liberation by means of:

committed and responsible action Karma,

leading a life of pragmatic, sensible wisdom Jnana,

being an ascetic, living solitary, meditative Yoga.

फलरूपत्वात् ॥ २६

phalarūpatvāt ॥ 26

फल–रूपत्वात् ॥ २६

फल–रूपत्वात् $^{n5/1}$ ॥

Theme 26 Why Bhakti?

26. Bhakti is heavenly and supreme, since it contains the fruits in its practice itself.

There is no external feedback needed, no time lag in experiencing the bliss, the abundance, the completeness.

ईश्वरस्याप्यभिमानद्वेषित्वाद् दैन्यप्रियत्वाच्च ॥ २७

īśvarasyāpyabhimānadveṣitvād dainyapriyatvācca
॥ 27

ईश्वरस्य अपि अभिमान-द्वेषित्वात् दैन्य-प्रियत्वात् च ॥ २७

ईश्वरस्य $^{m6/1}$ अपि ^{0} अभिमान-द्वेषित्वात् $^{n5/1}$

दैन्य-प्रियत्वात् $^{n5/1}$ च ^{0} ॥

Theme 27 Humility

27. The boss too takes kindly to humility and rejects vanity.

Any grace that showers is due to an attitude of supplication rather than onerous display of skill.

तस्या ज्ञानमेव साधनमित्येके ॥ २८

tasyā jñānameva sādhanamityeke ॥ 28

तस्याः ज्ञानम् एव साधनम् इत्येके ॥ २८

तस्याः $^{f6/1}$ इत्येके^{0} ज्ञानम्$^{n2/1}$ एव^0 साधनम्$^{n2/1}$ (मन्यन्ते) $^{लट्\,iii/3}$ ॥

Some opine Jnana alone is the means to Bhakti.

अन्योन्याश्रयत्वमित्यन्ये ॥ २९

anyonyāśrayatvamityanye ॥ 29

अन्योन्य आश्रयत्वम् इत्यन्ये ॥ २९

इत्यन्ये ^{0} आश्रयत्वम् $^{n1/1}$ अन्योन्य ^{0} (मन्यन्ते) $^{लट्\,iii/3}$ ॥

SomeOthers opine Bhakti is based on Jnana and Seva both.

स्वयं फलरूपतेति ब्रह्मकुमाराः ॥ ३०

svayaṃphalarūpateti brahmakumārāḥ ॥ 30

स्वयम् फल–रूपता इति ब्रह्मकुमाराः ॥ ३०

ब्रह्मकुमाराः $^{m1/3}$ फल–रूपता $^{n3/1}$ स्वयम् $^{n2/1}$ इति ^{0} (मन्यन्ते) $^{लट्\,iii/3}$ ॥

The four child sages viz. Sanaka, Sanandana, Sanatana and Sanatkumara; and Narada; all who are sons of Lord Brahma; opine Bhakti is its own delightful means and reward as well.

Theme 28-30 Bhakti Paths

28., 29., 30. The wise have many views regarding Bhakti.

A thorough understanding of the principles is considered as helpful in devotion by some.

Some others have the view that both wisdom and honest work have a harmonious mix in Bhakti.

Narada and the Kumars think that expressing love intensely is the sole means as well as the gain.

राजगृहभोजनादिषु तथैव दृष्टत्वात् ॥ ३१

न तेन राजपरितोषः क्षुधाशान्तिर्वा ॥ ३२

rājagṛhabhojanādiṣu tathaiva dṛṣṭatvāt ॥ 31

na tena rājaparitoṣaḥ kṣudhāśāntirvā ॥ 32

राजगृह-भोजन-आदिषु तथैव दृष्टत्वात् ॥ ३१

राजगृह-भोजन-आदिषु $^{m7/3}$ तथैव ^{0} दृष्टत्वात् $^{n5/1}$ ॥

As an illustration consider the examples of a royal palace, sumptuous food, etc.

न तेन राज–परितोषः क्षुधा–शान्तिः वा ॥ ३२

न ^{0} तेन $^{m3/1}$ राज–परितोषः $^{m1/1}$ क्षुधा–शान्तिः $^{m1/1}$ वा ^{0} ॥

Not by a palace alone is a kingdom made, nor is by the sight of delicacies alone is the hunger satiated.

Theme 31-32 Experiential Importance

31., 32. It strongly behoves the aspirant to work intensely on the path of Bhakti.

Just by thinking or listening it doesn't materialize. Dreaming alone doesn't get you anywhere, getting up and putting it in action is needed.

A real divine experience is a must on the path. That alone is the guide as well as the fuel.

तस्मात् सैव ग्राह्या मुमुक्षुभिः ॥ ३३

tasmāt saiva grāhyā mumukṣubhiḥ ॥ 33

तस्मात् सा एव ग्राह्या मुमुक्षुभिः ॥ ३३

तस्मात् [0] सा [f1/1] एव [0] ग्राह्या [f3/1] मुमुक्षुभिः [m3/3] ॥

Theme 33 Pure Bliss

33. Hence that experience of pure bliss should be earnestly sought for by the aspirants.

Am I on track? Will my efforts lead me home? What is the proof that my Sadhana is proper?

Narada answers all such misgivings and doubts by posing a question:
Did you have any honest fulfilling experience in your pursuits at any time or is there a total blank?

Did you actually experience Freedom, Protection, undiluted Joy, a strong sense of Purity … ?

तस्याः साधनानि गायन्त्याचार्याः ॥ ३४

tasyāḥ sādhanāni gāyantyācāryāḥ ॥ 34

तस्याः साधनानि गायन्ति आचार्याः ॥ ३४

तस्याः$^{f6/1}$ आचार्याः$^{m1/3}$ साधनानि$^{n2/3}$ गायन्ति$^{लट्\ iii/3}$ ॥

Theme 34 Compassion of the Guru

34. Wise masters describe the proper ways to be on the PATH.

Basic guidelines are judiciously explained and taught with caring. These will be of utmost benefit to the seekers.

तच्तु विषयत्यागात् सङ्गत्यागाच्च ॥ ३५

tattu viṣayatyāgātsaṅgatyāgācca ॥ 35

तत् तु विषय–त्यागात् सङ्ग–त्यागात् च ॥ ३५

तत् $^{n1/1}$ तु ^{0} विषय–त्यागात् $^{m5/1}$ सङ्ग–त्यागात् $^{m5/1}$ च ^{0}

(सम्भवेत् $^{वि०लि० iii/1}$) ॥

Firstly that would be made possible by dropping petty matters and transitory attachments.

Theme 35 How is Devotion to be had?

35. On the PATH, the starting guideline is to observe and shy away from any activity that is composed of meanness, weakness, helplessness, wastefulness …

अव्यावृत्तभजनात् ॥ ३६

avyāvṛttabhajanāt ॥ 36

अव्यावृत्त-भजनात् ॥ ३६

अव्यावृत्त-भजनात् $^{m5/1}$ ॥

By uninterrupted service to humanity.

Theme 36 Active Social Service

36. When one has identified and forsaken activities that were not at all productive, then one should start devoting time to social service.

Service is a key aspect of Bhakti. Social service is not only service to strangers. Rather it begins at home.

Firstly personal Sadhana is a Service. Start helping out at home to make the family evolve and be useful to friends. Reach out to the neighbourhood. Find out some worldwide projects that align with your temperament.

Tireless and intense service for oneself and the world at large. Consider a Mother. She ain't afraid of anyone or anything 'cause she is caring for someone.

लोकेऽपि भगवद्गुणश्रवणकीर्तनात् ॥ ३७

loke'pi bhagavadguṇaśravaṇakīrtanāt ॥ 37

लोके अपि भगवत्-गुण-श्रवण-कीर्तनात् ॥ ३७

लोके ^{m7/1} अपि ⁰ भगवत्-गुण-श्रवण-कीर्तनात् ^{m5/1} ॥

Even in ordinary day to day life by listening about the Divine and talking and singing his praises.

भगवत्-गुण -> भगवद्गुण ǀ Consonant Sandhi
8.4.53 झलां जश् झशि ǀ

Theme 37 Revere and Glorify Divinity

37. Many times we wonder if talking about God is desirable? We hesitate to equate TRUTH, HONESTY, PURITY, KINDNESS, HUMILITY to the Divine. We have unspoken or vague notions perhaps.

Secularism is taken to mean correctness, but what exactly is it?

Narada unequivocally says that the aspirant must take the Lord's name. On the path we must sing His praises. We must recount His adventures.

Unhesitatingly call upon the Lord. Think He is very near to you. Interact with Him in simple ways that reflect authenticity and purity.

मुख्यतस्तु महत्कृपयैव भगवत्कृपालेशाद्वा ॥ ३८

mukhyatastu mahatkṛpayaiva
bhagavatkṛpāleśādvā ॥ 38

मुख्यतः तु महत्–कृपया एव भगवत्–कृपा–लेशात् वा ॥ ३८

मुख्यतः ^{0} तु ^{0} महत्–कृपया $^{f3/1}$ एव ^{0} भगवत्–कृपा–लेशात् $^{m5/1}$
वा ^{0} ॥

However, primarily Bhakti is due to great blessing, or
by a drop of divine grace.

Theme 38 Grace is the Key

38. Know the golden principle.

It is to keep up with your efforts, but know that Bhakti develops only when the Lord is pleased. We can never equate our efforts or skills or intelligence to His Grace. His grace may also reflect in the blessing received from a great soul in some chance meeting.

Not at any time can one logically deduce why a miracle happened. How some fortune came our way. Why did lady luck shower beatitude…

महत्सङ्गस्तु दुर्लभोऽगम्योऽमोघश्च ॥ ३९

mahatsaṅgastu durlabho'gamyo'moghaśca ॥ 39

महत्-सङ्गः तु दुर्लभः अगम्यः अमोघः च ॥ ३९

महत् सङ्गः $^{m1/1}$ तु ^{0} दुर्लभः $^{m1/1}$ अगम्यः $^{m1/1}$ अमोघः $^{m1/1}$ च ^{0} ॥

Again, the company of a great soul is extremely rare. Also, the effects of such company are hard to deduce logically, yet infallible.

Theme 39 Tough to get the Guru

39. Gurus and Masters and Blessers are rarer than you think. And one can never fathom a Guru's ways.

The Master might suggest Ayurveda to one, Allopathy to another and Homeopathy to a third.

I may be given gardening that isn't to my liking, she may be given reception that is not her cup of tea, he may be asked to serve in the kitchen that is very much up his sleeve!

लभ्यतेऽपि तत्कृपयैव ॥ ४०

labhyate'pi tatkṛpayaiva ॥ 40

लभ्यते अपि तत्-कृपया एव ॥ ४०

तत्-कृपया ^f3/1   एव ^0   अपि ^0   लभ्यते ^लट् कर्म० iii/1 ॥

Suffice to reiterate that grace alone invokes Bhakti.

Theme 40 Lord's Darshan

40. Emphasized again that the Bhakti that leads to liberation is the result of blessing received from a noble soul which is in fact the touch of God.

That is why Indians are so fervent of having the good Lord's vision and darshan.

तस्मिंस्तज्जने भेदाभावात् ॥ ४१

tasmiṃstajjane bhedābhāvāt ॥ 41

तस्मिन् तत्–जने भेद्–अभावात् ॥ ४१

तस्मिन् $^{m7/1}$ तत्–जने $^{m7/1}$ भेद्–अभावात् $^{m5/1}$ ॥

In Him and His devotee there isn't any difference.

Theme 41 Lord and Devotee are one

41. A point that escapes the conviction of many aspirants who fail to find the PATH is - The Lord lives inside His Bhakta.

All scriptures give the idea that pure souls are God's instruments.

Still many seekers fail to make it since they are trying to fit God into some concept. They have a mistaken belief that the INFINITY is one that aligns with some definition they have in their head. So they are unable to turn to someone who does not exactly match! In fact one hears the phrase commonly – He too gets angry, he too needs food to eat, she too applies make-up, so how can they be GOD?

Definitely not a chance of the LORD befitting a notion. Or perhaps He might. Ha!

So turn to the Sangha. Align yourself with a Satsang. And slowly something shall blossom forth.

तदेव साध्यतां तदेव साध्यताम् ॥ ४२

tadeva sādhyatāṃ tadeva sādhyatām ॥ 42

तद्-एव साध्यताम् तद्-एव साध्यताम् ॥ ४२

तद्-एव ^{0} साध्यताम् $^{लोट्\ iii/1}$ तद्-एव ^{0} साध्यताम् $^{लोट्\ iii/1}$ ॥

That alone one must strive for, that alone must be
the aim.

Theme 42 Satsang is worth every bit

42. Finding the proper company should be the prime aim for the aspirant. Unless he talks and interacts, unless he drinks the nectar of devotion, how can he proceed on the PATH?

Satsang is very important. Find one in your area and be regular in attending it. It shall surely uplift you.

दुःसङ्गः सर्वथैव त्याज्यः ॥ ४३

duḥsaṅgaḥ sarvathaiva tyājyaḥ ॥ 43

दुःसङ्गः सर्वथा एव त्याज्यः ॥ ४३

दुःसङ्गः $^{m1/1}$ सर्वथा ^{0} एव ^{0} त्याज्यः $^{m1/1}$ ॥

Shun evil company at all cost.

Theme 43 Shun bad company

43. Immediately cut away from the wrong person. Stop meeting him or phoning him forthwith. Do not wait. Do not tarry.

The stain of the foul is rather hard to will away and takes eons to wash clean.

कामक्रोधमोहस्मृतिभ्रंशबुद्धिनाशसर्वनाशकारणत्वात् ॥ ४४

kāmakrodhamohasmṛtibhraṃśabuddhināśasarva
nāśakāraṇatvāt ॥ 44

काम-क्रोध-मोह-स्मृतिभ्रंश-बुद्धिनाश-सर्वनाश-कारणत्वात् ॥ ४४

काम-क्रोध-मोह-स्मृतिभ्रंश-बुद्धिनाश-सर्वनाश-कारणत्वात् [n5/1] ॥

That being the cause for wanton desire, unfulfilled desire leading to anger, that in turn to delusion, that in turn causing loss of memory of right and wrong, that making the intellect take a destructive decision, which is the cause for total annihilation.

Theme 44 Nip the Evil in the Bud

44. Our mind is a complex entity. Our brain takes years to groom. Destructive habits cannot be wished away, they form easily but almost never break.

तरङ्गायिता अपीमे सङ्गात्समुद्रायन्ति ॥ ४५

taraṅgāyitā apīme saṅgātsamudrāyanti ॥ 45

तरङ्गायिताः अपि इमे सङ्गात् समुद्रायन्ति ॥ ४५

तरङ्गायिताः $^{m1/3}$ इमे $^{m1/3}$ अपि ^{0} सङ्गात् $^{m5/1}$
समुद्रायन्ति $^{लट् \, iii/3}$ ॥

Since these ripples (of evil associations) collect together and become a formidable ocean.

Theme 45 Drop by drop it Overflows

45. Drop by drop a pot is filled.

Slowly one day a habit cultivated absent-mindedly becomes a force to reckon with, and can destroy one completely.

कस्तरति कस्तरति मायाम् ?

यः सङ्गांस्त्यजति यो महानुभावं सेवते निर्ममो भवति ॥ ४६

kastarati kastarati māyām ? yassaṅgāṃstyajati yo
mahānubhāvaṃ sevate nirmamo bhavati ॥ 46

कः तरति कः तरति मायाम् ?

यः सङ्गान् त्यजति यः महान्–उभावम् सेवते निर्ममः भवति ॥ ४६

कः ^{m1/1} तरति ^{लट् iii/1} ? कः ^{m1/1} मायाम् ^{f2/1} तरति ^{लट् iii/1} ?

यः ^{m1/1} सङ्गान् ^{m2/3} त्यजति ^{लट् iii/1}

यः ^{m1/1} महान्–उभावम् ^{m1/1} सेवते ^{लट् iii/1}

निर्ममः ^{m1/1} भवति ^{लट् iii/1} ॥

Who crosses over? Who sails free of mishap?

The one who forthwith drops evil company.

The one who devotedly seeks and serves the noble.

The one who does not get entangled and caught up
in emotions, trifles, or false notions.

Theme 46 Qualities of the Devotee

46. Of all souls, a devotee is one who exhibits special traits.

Who do you think is a devotee poses Narada. *And immediately answers*, of course the one who crosses over the ocean of bondage.

And Narada asks further, who is the one who fords the stormy river? Who keeps his balance amidst the terror thrown up every day (by the mind, the memory, the lurking desires)?

Stop. Become Still. Untangle your thoughts.
Go out and seek the TRUTH.

Steve Jobs spent time with Himalayan Saints.
Mark Zuckerberg sought blessings at Neem Karoli Baba's ashram in Kainchi, Nainital.

यो विविक्तस्थानं सेवते यो लोकबन्धमुन्मूलयति निस्त्रैगुण्यो भवति योगक्षेमं त्यजति ॥ ४७

yo viviktasthānaṃ sevate yo
lokabandhamunmūlayati nistraiguṇyo bhavati
yogakṣemaṃ tyajati ॥ 47

यः विविक्त–स्थानम् सेवते यः लोकबन्धम् उन्मूलयति निस्त्रै–गुण्यः भवति योग–क्षेमम् त्यजति ॥ ४७

यः $^{m1/1}$ विविक्त–स्थानम् $^{n2/1}$ सेवते $^{लट् iii/1}$

यः $^{m1/1}$ लोकबन्धम् $^{m2/1}$ उन्मूलयति $^{लट् iii/1}$

निस्त्रै–गुण्यः $^{m2/3}$ भवति $^{लट् iii/1}$

योग–क्षेमम् $^{m2/1}$ त्यजति $^{लट् iii/1}$ ॥

One who seeks solitude, meditation, going within;

One who strives to vanquish lust and greed;

One who balances lifestyle.

One who quells the need to hoard and amass.

Theme 47 Meditation

47. Meditation is not just sitting with eyes closed. Meditation is much more than that.

A harmony within is meditation. Paring and Pruning one's endless desires is meditation.

यः कर्मफलं त्यजति कर्माणि संन्यस्यति ततो निर्द्वन्द्वो भवति ॥ ४८

yaḥ karmaphalaṃ tyajati karmāṇi saṃnyasyati
tato nirdvandvo bhavati ॥ 48

यः कर्मफलम् त्यजति कर्माणि संन्यस्यति ततः निर्द्वन्द्वः भवति ॥ ४८

यः ^{m1/1}   कर्मफलम् ^{n2/1} त्यजति ^{लट् iii/1}

कर्माणि ^{m2/3} संन्यस्यति ^{लट् iii/1}

ततः ⁰ निर्द्वन्द्वः ^{m1/1} भवति ^{लट् iii/1} ॥

One who drops the feverishness for a quick result;

One who detaches from taking credits;

Then that one becomes free of mishap and blame.

Theme 48 Drop the Feverishness

48. Accidents are not just a coincidence.
Disease is not only from infection.

Many a mistake is knowingly made and repeated,
many a disaster has been silently nurtured.

वेदानपि संन्यस्यति केवलमविच्छिन्नानुरागं लभते ॥ ४९

vedānapi saṃnyasyati
kevalamavicchinnānurāgaṃ labhate ॥ 49

वेदान् अपि संन्यस्यति केवलम् अविच्छिन्न–अनुरागम् लभते ॥ ४९

वेदान् ^m2/3 अपि ^0 संन्यस्यति ^लृट् iii/1

केवलम् ^m2/1 अविच्छिन्न–अनुरागम् ^m2/1 लभते ^लृट् iii/1 ॥

Moreover,

One who renounces the pride of scholarships;

Derives unmitigated, unstained happiness.

104

Theme 49 Pride is worth Renouncing

49. One's head becomes a heavy load to carry, if it is stuffed with pride.

स तरति स तरति स लोकांस्तारयति ॥ ५०

sa tarati sa tarati sa lokāṃstārayati ॥ 50

सः तरति सः तरति सः लोकान् तारयति ॥ ५०

सः $^{m1/1}$ तरति $^{लट्\ iii/1}$

सः $^{m1/1}$ तरति $^{लट्\ iii/1}$

सः $^{m1/1}$ लोकान् $^{m2/3}$ तारयति $^{लट्\ iii/1}$ ॥

He crosses the finishing line;

He sails across storms and hurdles;

He helps, teaches, enlightens common people too.

Theme 50 Enlightenment is Beautiful

50. Enlightenment is beautiful.

When one learns how to cross the river,
automatically without thinking , one begins to help
others do the same.

अनिर्वचनीयं प्रेमस्वरूपम् ॥ ५१

anirvacanīyaṃ premasvarūpam ॥ 51

अनिर्‌–वचनीयम् प्रेम–स्वरूपम् ॥ ५१

अनिर्‌–वचनीयम्$^{n1/1}$ प्रेम–स्वरूपम्$^{n1/1}$ (अस्ति $^{लट्\ iii/1}$) ॥

Devotion is like Love that is beyond words.

Theme 51 A Love beyond SpaceTime

51. Our space time is a heady mix. It expresses in sound, language and communication.

But Bhakti is something else again. Not altogether is it defined by the laws of creation, nor is it limited.

मूकास्वादनवत् ॥ ५२

mūkāsvādanavat ॥ 52

मूका–आस्वादनवत् ॥ ५२

मूका–आस्वादनवत्$^{n1/1}$ ॥

Bhakti cannot be expressed in words, just as the experience of a delicious taste cannot be spoken of by a dumb person.

Theme 52 An inexpressible Taste

52. Of the many tales that can be told, Bhakti chooses to be elusive in that though experiential, no words pop out, only the countenance glows.

प्रकाश्यते क्वापि पात्रे ॥ ५३

prakāśyate kvāpi pātre ॥ 53

प्रकाश्यते क्वापि पात्रे ॥ ५३

क्वापि ^{0} पात्रे $^{m7/1}$ (सा $^{f1/1}$) प्रकाश्यते $^{लट्\ कर्म°\ iii/1}$ ॥

In any receptacle or recipient at any time that Bhakti
can shine forth from.

Theme 53 Bhakti comes a calling

53. Not only good men and women, not only children and old sages, but that grace can strike even the seemingly ignorant or dull-witted.

Grace can dawn in a robber or an absconder.

Even an Animal or a Tree.

गुणरहितं कामनारहितं प्रतिक्षणवर्धमानमविच्छिन्नं
सूक्ष्मतरमनुभवरूपम् ॥ ५४

guṇarahitaṃ kāmanārahitaṃ
pratikṣaṇavardhamānamavicchinnaṃ
sūkṣmataramanubhavarūpam ॥ 54

गुण–रहितम् कामना–रहितम् प्रतिक्षण–वर्धमानम् अविच्छिन्नम्
सूक्ष्मतरम्–अनुभव–रूपम् ॥ ५४
(सा $^{f1/1}$) गुण–रहितम् $^{n2/1}$ कामना–रहितम् $^{n2/1}$
प्रतिक्षण–वर्धमानम् $^{n2/1}$ अविच्छिन्नम् $^{n2/1}$
सूक्ष्मतरम् $^{n2/1}$ अनुभव–रूपम् $^{n2/1}$ (अस्ति $^{लट् iii/1}$) ॥

That Bhakti is devoid of polarity, free from selfish
motive, throbbing every moment, unmitigated, quite
subtle and of the nature of inner experience.

Theme 54 Devotion is Palpable

54. Devotion is a Purity that may be manifest outwardly, or it may be hidden within.

One thing is sure, it colors every cell and pore of the being.

तत्प्राप्य तदेवावलोकयति तदेव शृणोति तदेव भाषयति तदेव चिन्तयति ॥ ५५

tatprāpya tadevāvalokayati tadeva śṛṇoti tadeva bhāṣayati tadeva cintayati ॥ 55

तत्–प्राप्य तदेव अवलोकयति तदेव शृणोति तदेव भाषयति तदेव चिन्तयति ॥ ५५

तत्–प्राप्य ल्यप् ० तदेव ० अवलोकयति लट् iii/1 तदेव ० शृणोति लट् iii/1 तदेव ० भाषयति लट् iii/1 तदेव ० चिन्तयति लट् iii/1 ॥

That Bhakti having attained, the Bhakta sees only devotees all around, he hears only devotees everywhere, only devotion he expresses and only devotion he mulls of.

Theme 55 All is Well

55. A great quality of the devotee is that he goes by the maxim – ALL IS WELL.

गौणी त्रिधा गुणभेदादार्तादिभेदाद्वा ॥ ५६

gauṇī tridhā guṇabhedādārtādibhedādvā ॥ 56

गौणी त्रिधा गुण–भेदात् आर्त–आदि–भेदात् वा ॥ ५६

गौणी [f1/1]   त्रिधा [f1/1]

गुण–भेदात् [5/1]   आर्त–आदि–भेदात् [5/1]   वा [0] ॥

Inferior devotion may be classified as of three types; based on the triCreative natural energies of Sattva, Rajas and Tamas; or based on the quality of the aspirant; viz. the distressed seeking relief, the ambitious seeking wealth and the awakened seeking god realization.

Theme 56 Gradations of apara Bhakti

56. So far the para Bhakti has been discussed. Para meaning supreme. Ideal. Actual. Pure.

Here Narada gives a glimpse of the apara Bhakti. Or the Bhakti that isn't really Bhakti. However since the true Bhakti is rare, Narada thought of giving hints to the seekers at what stage they are.

Refer Bhagavad Gita 7.16

चतुर्विधा भजन्ते माम् , जनास् सुकृतिनोऽर्जुन ।
आर्तो जिज्ञासुर् अर्थार्थी , ज्ञानी च भरतर्षभ ॥ ७.१६

उत्तरस्मादुत्तरस्मात्पूर्वपूर्वा श्रेयाय भवति ॥ ५७

uttarasmāduttarasmātpūrvapūrvā śreyāya bhavati
॥ 57

उत्तरस्मात् उत्तरस्मात् पूर्व–पूर्वा श्रेयाय भवति ॥ ५७

उत्तरस्मात् $^{5/1}$ उत्तरस्मात् $^{5/1}$ पूर्व–पूर्वा $^{f1/1}$ श्रेयाय $^{आय\,0}$
भवति $^{ऌट्\,iii/1}$ ॥

(With reference to the previous verse 56):
That which comes earlier is higher than that which
follows, and vice versa.

Theme 57 Truth Ambition Prayer

57. Thus Sattvic Bhakti is far better than Rajasic Bhakti, which is much more desirable than Tamasic Bhakti.

Conversely it applies to the other clause; viz., the Bhakti of the distressed is inferior to that of the ambitious, which again is inferior to the awakened.

अन्यस्मात् सौलभ्यं भक्तौ ॥ ५८

anyasmāt saulabhyaṃ bhaktau ॥ 58

अन्यस्मात् सौलभ्यम् भक्तौ ॥ ५८

अन्यस्मात् ^{0} सौलभ्यम् $^{n2/1}$ भक्तौ $^{f7/1}$ ॥

Compared to other lifestyles, success or attainment of the highest bliss comes rather easily in a devotional lifestyle.

Theme 58 Superiority of Bhakti

58. Even though one may be struggling in a form of apara Bhakti, whether 3rd grade or 2nd grade, still by being devoted to some ideal, one will sooner or later taste some success. And quickly move up the ladder.

प्रमाणान्तरस्यानपेक्षत्वात् स्वयं प्रमाणत्वात् ॥ ५९

pramāṇāntarasyānapekṣatvāt svayaṃ
pramāṇatvāt ॥ 59

प्रमाण–अन्तरस्य अनपेक्षत्वात् स्वयम् प्रमाणत्वात् ॥ ५९

प्रमाण–अन्तरस्य $^{m6/1}$ अनपेक्षत्वात् $^{m5/1}$ स्वयम् ^{0}
प्रमाणत्वात् $^{m5/1}$ ॥

Since instead of depending on external feedback, a
devotional lifestyle is its own inbuilt proof.

Theme 59 Slow and Steady

59. Being steadfast in an occupation or being devoted to a cause has a healthy success rate.

शान्तिरूपात् परमानन्दरूपाच्च ॥ ६०

śāntirūpāt paramānandarūpācca ॥ 60

शान्तिरूपात् परमानन्दरूपाच्च ॥ ६०

शान्ति-रूपात् $^{n5/1}$ परमानन्द-रूपात् $^{n5/1}$ च ^{0} ॥

Considering it stems from peace and ingrains a contented happy living.

Theme 60 Devotion nurtures Peace

60. Peace is Bliss and Bliss is in Peace.

लोकहानौ चिन्ता न कार्या निवेदितात्मलोकवेदत्वात् ॥ ६१

lokahānau cintā na kāryā niveditātmalokavedatvāt
॥ 61

लोक-हानौ चिन्ता न कार्या निवेदित-आत्म-लोक-वेदत्वात् ॥ ६१

लोक-हानौ f7/1 चिन्ता f1/1 न 0 कार्या ऋ f1/1 निवेदित-आत्म-
लोक-वेदत्वात् n5/1 ॥

A devotee suffers no qualms as he doesn't see any
misery in the world whatsoever. He has accepted the
Lord as the director of his soul, his worldly affairs,
and his achievements.

Theme 61 Escape from Misery

61. Why this? Why that? Why does it happen to me?

Obviously if you consider the world as belonging to some puny being, dictated by some despot, or keep observing flaws, focussing on the gloomy…

Then what a delight when your lose your spectacles.

न तत्सिद्धौ लोकव्यवहारो हेयः किन्तु फलत्यागस्तत्साधनं च कार्यमेव
॥ ६२

na tatsiddhau lokavyavahāro heyaḥ kintu
phalatyāgastatsādhanaṃ ca kāryameva ॥ 62

न तत्-सिद्धौ लोक-व्यवहारः हेयः किन्तु फल-त्यागः तत्-साधनम् च
कार्यम् एव ॥ ६२

तत्-सिद्धौ $^{f7/1}$ लोक-व्यवहारः $^{m1/1}$ न ^{0} हेयः $^{m1/1}$ किन्तु ^{0}
फल-त्यागः $^{m1/1}$ तत्-साधनम् $^{n2/1}$ च ^{0} कार्यम् $^{n2/1}$ एव ^{0} ॥

When Bhakti has blossomed within, one must not
forsake worldly duty or responsibility. Rather one
must drop the feverishness for quick results. And
continue one's efforts towards service and hard
work.

Theme 62 Caution to the Devotee

62. Even after reaching the TOP, continue toiling. Do not slacken. Maintain your discipline. Keep up your practices.

स्त्रीधननास्तिकवैरिचरित्रं न श्रवणीयम् ॥ ६३

strīdhananāstikavairicaritraṃ na śravaṇīyam ॥ 63

स्त्री-धन-नास्तिक-वैरि-चरित्रम् न श्रवणीयम् ॥ ६३

स्त्री-धन-नास्तिक-वैरि-चरित्रम् $^{n1/1}$ न ^{0} श्रवणीयम् $^{तव्यत् \, n1/1}$ ॥

On this path, one must lend no ear to conversations of lust, amassing wealth, stories of injustice or hatred.

Theme 63 Folly of Senses

63. The ear is mighty suspect. Hearing the wrong thing can crack the most beautiful relationship.

It has become a dictum –
See no Evil. Hear no Evil. Speak no Evil.

अभिमानदम्भादिकं त्याज्यम् ॥ ६४

abhimānadambhādikaṃ tyājyam ॥ 64

अभिमान-दम्भ-आदिकम् त्याज्यम् ॥ ६४

अभिमान-दम्भ-आदिकम् [n1/1]　त्याज्यम् [तव्यत् n1/1]　॥

One must abandon false pride, hypocrisy, etc.
forthwith.

Theme 64 In Vain is Hypocrisy

64. Though self-defeatist, vanity and hypocrisy rule the roost.

तदर्पिताखिलाचारः सन् कामक्रोधाभिमानादिकं तस्मिन्नेव करणीयम् ॥ ६५

tadarpitākhilācāraḥ san
kāmakrodhābhimānādikaṃ tasminneva
karaṇīyam ॥ 65

तत्-अर्पिता अखिल-आचारः सन् काम-क्रोध-अभिमान-आदिकम् तस्मिन् एव करणीयम् ॥ ६५

तत्-अर्पिता ^{क f1/1}   अखिल-आचारः ^{m1/3}   सन् ^{शतृ m1/1}

काम-क्रोध-अभिमान-आदिकम् ^{n1/1}   तस्मिन् ^{m7/1}   एव ⁰

करणीयम् ^{तव्यत् n1/1} ॥

Having offered all impulses to the Divine; Being
established within; one must feel the emotions of
lust, anger, false pride, etc. w.r.t Him alone.

Theme 65 Injunction to the Devotee

65. Make the Divine the target, not some limited being, and soon the shad-shatrus (six enemies within) weaken.

त्रिरूपभङ्गपूर्वकं नित्यदासनित्यकान्ताभजनात्मकं प्रेम कार्यं प्रेमैव कार्यम् ॥ ६६

trirūpabhaṅgapūrvakaṃ
nityadāsanityakāntābhajanātmakaṃ prem kāryaṃ
premaiva kāryam ॥ 66

त्रि-रूप-भङ्ग-पूर्वकम् नित्यदास-नित्यकान्ता-भजन-आत्मकम् प्रेम कार्यम् प्रेम एव कार्यम् ॥ ६६

त्रि-रूप-भङ्ग-पूर्वकम् $^{n1/1}$ नित्यदास-नित्यकान्ता-भजन-आत्मकम् $^{n1/1}$ प्रेम $^{n1/1}$ कार्यम् $^{n1/1}$ प्रेम $^{n1/1}$ एव ^{0} कार्यम् $^{n1/1}$ ॥

The earlier mentioned triCreative forces of nature must be overcome. Lovingly one must practice being in love only, like a devoted employee or a devoted lover, keeping the Lord in sight.

Theme 66 Love is Hard Work

66. Love endures when nurtured well.

Trust takes ages to develop. Faith is a life-long process.

भक्ता एकान्तिनो मुख्याः ॥ ६७

bhaktā ekāntino mukhyāḥ ॥ 67

भक्ताः एकान्तिनः मुख्याः ॥ ६७

भक्ताः [m1/3]   एकान्तिनः [m1/3]   मुख्याः [m1/3]   ॥

Amongst all devotees, those who are exclusive in
their devotion to the divine are the best.

Theme 67 Hone one Skill

67. You may be a jack of all trades, you might play two games well, however if you wish to reach the TOP, work on a single idea.

Refer Samadhi Pada of Patanjali Yoga Sutras

तत्प्रतिषेधार्थम् एकतत्त्वाभ्यासः । 1.32

कण्ठावरोधरोमाञ्चाश्रुभिः परस्परं लपमानाः पावयन्ति कुलानि पृथिवीं
च ॥ ६८

kaṇṭhāvarodharomāñcāśrubhiḥ parasparaṃ
lapamānāḥ pāvayanti kulāni pṛthivīṃ ca ॥ 68

कण्ठ-अवरोध-रोमाञ्च-अश्रुभिः परस्परम् लपमानाः पावयन्ति कुलानि
पृथिवीम् च ॥ ६८

(ते $^{m1/3}$) कण्ठ-अवरोध-रोमाञ्च-अश्रुभिः $^{n3/3}$ परस्परम् ^{0}
लपमानाः $^{शानच्\,1/3}$ कुलानि $^{n2/3}$ पृथिवीम् $^{f2/1}$ च ^{0}
पावयन्ति $^{लट्\,iii/3}$ ॥

With throats choked, eyes shedding tears of
gratefulness, body tingling with divine excitement;
narrating glorifying exploits of the divine to each
other; they purify themselves, their village and clan,
as well as lighten the burden of mother earth.

Theme 68 Results of Bhakti

68. Saints are much sought after for this…

तीर्थीकुर्वन्ति तीर्थानि सुकर्मीकुर्वन्ति कर्माणि सच्छास्त्रीकुर्वन्ति शास्त्राणि ॥ ६९

tīrthīkurvanti tīrthāni sukarmīkurvanti karmāṇi sacchāstrīkurvanti śāstrāṇi ॥ 69

तीर्थी-कुर्वन्ति तीर्थानि सुकर्मी-कुर्वन्ति कर्माणि सत्_-शास्त्री-कुर्वन्ति शास्त्राणि ॥ ६९

(ते $^{m1/3}$) तीर्थानि $^{n2/3}$ तीर्थी-कुर्वन्ति $^{लट् \, iii/3}$

कर्माणि $^{n2/3}$ सुकर्मी-कुर्वन्ति $^{लट् \, iii/3}$

शास्त्राणि $^{n2/3}$ सत्_-शास्त्री-कुर्वन्ति $^{लट् \, iii/3}$ ॥

(*From verse 68*)their narrations of the Lord's exploits; transforms towns into places of pilgrimage; mundane chores of life into sacred acts; and education and study becomes worthwhile.

Theme 69 Man makes the Tirtha

69. Ganges is divine. Stanford is sacrosanct.

Why? Countless devoted people. That's why.

तन्मयाः ॥ ७०

tanmayāḥ ॥ 70

तन्मयाः ॥ ७०
तन्मयाः m1/3 ॥

Their pores and cells are filled with His name, they
are completely absorbed in Him; whatever they may
be doing.

Theme 70 Bhaktas are Yogis

70. One who aligns his heart and soul,

whose intellect and senses are in sync,

who is devoted to his job,

QUALIFIES FOR BLISS.

मोदन्ते पितरो नृत्यन्ति देवताः सनाथा चेयं भूर्भवति ॥ ७१

modante pitaro nṛtyanti devatāḥ sanāthā ceyaṃ bhūrbhavati ॥ 71

मोदन्ते पितरः नृत्यन्ति देवताः सनाथा च इयम् भूः भवति ॥ ७१

पितरः ^{m1/3}   मोदन्ते ^{लट् iii/3}

देवताः ^{m1/3}   नृत्यन्ति ^{लट् iii/3}

सनाथा ^{f1/1} च ⁰ इयम् ^{f1/1} भूः ^{f1/1} भवति ^{लट् iii/1}   ॥

Forefathers and seniors citizens feel the delight;

Celebrities and famous personalities become

euphoric and dance; and

This blessed earth has finally a caring Sovereign.

Theme 71 Caring Monarch

71. Often the dilemma of citizens when going to vote is who shall provide good governance? Will we be taken care of and provided for?

This is succinctly answered here. The monarch is just your own amplification. He is the majority will in one body.

नास्ति तेषु जातिविद्यारूपकुलधनक्रियादिभेदः ॥ ७२

nāsti teṣu jātividyārūpakuladhanakriyādibhedaḥ ॥
72

नास्ति तेषु जाति-विद्या-रूप-कुल-धन-क्रिया-आदि-भेदः ॥ ७२

तेषु $^{m7/3}$ जाति-विद्या-रूप-कुल-धन-क्रिया-आदि-भेदः $^{m1/1}$

नास्ति $^{लट्\ iii/1}$ ॥

Amongst devotees there is not the slightest talk or
mention of race, educational qualification,
handsomeness, parentage, financial status,
occupation, etc.

Theme 72 Liberty Equality Fraternity

72. Only one aim powers a family. To begin with two people who make a couple. Raise children. Then it becomes a neighbourhood, society, state, and …

Sanity prevails in liberty, equality, fraternity. It is what all Nations aim for.

यतस्तदीयाः ॥ ७३

yatastadīyāḥ ॥ 73

यतः तदीयाः ॥ ७३

यतः ^{0} तदीयाः $^{m1/3}$ ॥

Since they all belong to Oneness, one world family.

Theme 73 One World Family

73. Our planet. EARTH. A bluish ball. A melting pot.

A place for all. All can be.

वादो नावलम्ब्यः ॥ ७४

vādo nāvalambyaḥ ॥ 74

वादः न अवलम्ब्यः ॥ ७४

वादः $^{m1/1}$ न ^{0} अवलम्ब्यः $^{तव्यत्\ m1/1}$ ॥

Be wary of entering into dispute or criticism or
comparison or argument over devotion, religion or
spiritual activity.

Theme 74 Do not Contend

74. Even though it is the easiest thing to do…

बाहुल्यावकाशादनियतत्वाच ॥ ७५

bāhulyāvakāśādaniyatatvācca ॥ 75

बाहुल्य-अवकाशात् अनियतत्वात् च ॥ ७५

बाहुल्य-अवकाशात् $^{m5/1}$ अनियतत्वात् $^{m5/1}$ च ^{0} ॥

(from verse 74) Devotional or religious activity should not be commented upon:

Due to the multiplicity of leisurely differing opinions that cannot be drawn to any logical conclusion.

Theme 75 We are all Different

75. Respect the diversity, honor the variety, and touch base with divinity.

भक्तिशास्त्राणि मननीयानि तदुद्बोधककर्माण्यपि करणीयानि ॥ ७६

bhaktiśāstrāṇi mananīyāni

tadudbodhakakarmāṇyapi karaṇīyāni ॥ 76

भक्ति-शास्त्राणि मननीयानि तत्–उद्-बोधक-कर्माणि अपि करणीयानि ॥ ७६

भक्ति-शास्त्राणि $^{n2/3}$ मननीयानि $^{अनीयर् \, n1/3}$ तत्–उद्-बोधक-कर्माणि $^{n2/3}$ अपि ^{0} करणीयानि $^{अनीयर् \, n1/3}$ ॥

One must give due thought and attention to the learning of devotional service. Also one must then put into practice the teaching diligently and with due respect.

Theme 76 Education and Practice

76. Proper education is the basic foundation. And it bears fruit only after sustained effort in the right direction.

सुखदुःखेच्छालाभादित्यक्ते काले प्रतीक्षमाणे क्षणार्धमपि व्यर्थं न नेयम्
॥ ७७

sukhaduḥkhecchālābhādityakte kāle
pratīkṣamāṇe kṣaṇārdhamapi vyarthaṃ na neyam
॥ 77

सुख-दुःख-इच्छा-लाभ-आदि-त्यक्ते काले प्रतीक्षमाणे क्षण-अर्धम् अपि
व्यर्थम् न नेयम् ॥ ७७

सुख-दुःख-इच्छा-लाभ-आदि-त्यक्ते ^{क्त m1/3}   काले ^{m7/1}
प्रतीक्षमाणे ^{शानच् n7/1}   क्षण-अर्धम् ^{n2/1}   अपि ⁰   व्यर्थम् ^{n2/1}   न ⁰
नेयम् ^{तव्यत् n1/1}   ॥

Having gotten over mundane hankerings for comfort,
material gain and wish fulfillment ; and having
pushed troubles and turmoil out of focus; in due time
having waited patiently enough for the mind to turn
towards a noble ideal; one must not lose even a
moment to delve into devotional service when the
call comes.

Theme 77 Timing is Everything

77. Whether sports or business or strategy, entertainment or catching a flight, life is largely influenced by TIME.

अहिंसासत्यशौचदयास्तिक्यादिचारित्र्याणि परिपालनीयानि ॥ ७८

ahiṃsāsatyaśaucadayāstikyādicāritryāṇi
paripālanīyāni ॥ 78

अहिंसा-सत्य-शौच-दया-आस्तिक्य-आदि-चारित्र्याणि परिपालनीयानि ॥ ७८

अहिंसा-सत्य-शौच-दया-आस्तिक्य-आदि-चारित्र्याणि n2/3
परिपालनीयानि अनीयर् n1/3 ॥

The virtues of Ahimsa, Truthfulness, physical and emotional Cleanliness, Kindness, Trust and so on must be thoroughly ingrained in one's character; so as to live a life of perfect devotion.

162

Theme 78 Ingredients of Devotion

78. Often one wonders – How did they achieve greatness?

सर्वदा सर्वभावेन निश्चिन्तैर्भगवानेव भजनीयः ॥ ७९

sarvadā sarvabhāvena niścintairbhagavāneva
bhajanīyaḥ ॥ 79

सर्वदा सर्व-भावेन निश्चिन्तैः भगवान् एव भजनीयः ॥ ७९

सर्वदा [0] सर्व-भावेन [m3/1] निश्चिन्तैः [m3/3] भगवान् [m1/1] एव [0] भजनीयः [अनीयर् m1/1] ॥

With complete involvement and feeling,
keeping aside mental distractions, always
the Divine and High ideal must be given top priority.

Theme 79 Prioritize

79. A key ingredient of growth, a vital factor in managing time and resources, of achieving the hard to get result, is…

Separate out the thoughts in the mind. Organize the to do lists. Plan, Design, Choose the best alternative and give your 100%.

स कीर्त्यमानः शीघ्रमेवाविर्भवति अनुभावयति च भक्तान् ॥ ८०

sa kīrtyamānaḥ śīghramevāvirbhavati
anubhāvayati ca bhaktān ॥ 80

सः कीर्त्यमानः शीघ्रम् एव आविर्भवति अनुभावयति च भक्तान् ॥ ८०
सः ^{m1/1} कीर्त्यमानः ^{शानच् m1/1} शीघ्रम् ⁰ एव ⁰ भक्तान् ^{m2/3}
आविर्भवति ^{ऌट् iii/1} अनुभावयति ^{ऌट् iii/1} च ⁰ ॥

The Lord responds quickly to cheerful praising,
materializes forthwith and gives an experience of
ultimate bliss to the devotees.

Theme 80 Cheer and Praise

80. What is the one attitude that shall get you there? That guarantees success?

This is it.

त्रिसत्यस्य भक्तिरेव गरीयसी भक्तिरेव गरीयसी ॥ ८१

trisatyasya bhaktireva garīyasī bhaktireva garīyasī
॥ 81

त्रि-सत्यस्य भक्तिः एव गरीयसी भक्तिः एव गरीयसी ॥ ८१

त्रि-सत्यस्य ^{n6/1} भक्तिः ^{f1/1} एव ⁰ गरीयसी ^{f1/1} भक्तिः ^{f1/1} एव ⁰ गरीयसी ^{f1/1} ॥

Of the three paths to wisdom, Karma-Jnana-Bhakti,
undoubtedly Bhakti is the greatest, loving devotion
alone is the perfect choice for many.

Theme 81 Karma Jnana Bhakti

81. Karma – Responsible Action can give you freedom, Jnana – Proper Knowledge can enlighten you, Bhakti – soulful loving devotion is supremely practical for most, and hence takes the cake.

In any path there will certainly be a mix of the other two. This fact is also highlighted here. For a path to lead to the supreme truth; hard work, proper vision and an attitude of cheerfulness; all go hand in hand.

गुणमाहात्म्यासक्तिरूपासक्तिपूजासक्तिस्मरणासक्तिदास्यासक्तिसख्यास
क्तिवात्सल्यासक्तिकान्तासक्त्यात्मनिवेदनासक्तितन्मयतासक्तिपरमविर
हासक्तिरूपा एकधाप्येकादशधा भवति ॥ ८२

guṇamāhātmyāsaktirūpāsaktipūjāsaktismaraṇāsa
ktidāsyāsaktisakhyāsaktivātsalyāsaktikāntāsaktyā
tmanivedanāsaktitanmayatāsaktiparamavirahāsak
tirūpā ekadhāpyekādaśadhā bhavati ॥ 82

गुणमाहात्म्यासक्ति-रूपासक्ति-पूजासक्ति-स्मरणासक्ति-दास्यासक्ति-
सख्यासक्ति-वात्सल्यासक्ति-कान्तासक्ति-आत्मनिवेदनासक्ति-
तन्मयतासक्ति-परमविरहासक्ति-रूपाः एकधा अपि एकादशधा भवति
॥ ८२

गुणमाहात्म्यासक्ति-रूपासक्ति-पूजासक्ति-स्मरणासक्ति-दास्यासक्ति-
सख्यासक्ति-वात्सल्यासक्ति--कान्ता-आसक्ति--आत्मनिवेदनासक्ति-
तन्मयतासक्ति-परमविरहासक्ति-रूपाः ^{ऌद् 1/3} एकधा ⁰ अपि ⁰
एकादशधा ⁰ भवति ^{ऌद् iii/1} ॥

आसक्ति feeling of oneness, total identification.

Bhakti though it is a single term, is seen in the world
in various expressions. Eleven common types of
Bhakti are noted, viz.

Theme 82 Bhakti as per temperament

82. 1) Praising the Lord's great virtues e.g. singing, 2) Drinking in the beauty of nature e.g. painting, 3) Being engrossed in prayer e.g. religious practices, 4) Remembering the positive in life e.g. optimism, 5) Being a trustworthy employee, 6) Being a true friend to someone, 7) Being a caring guardian to someone, 8) Being in love for someone or something, 9) Being absolutely humble in life, 10) Being wholly immersed in any activity, 11) Experiencing an insatiable and unbearable longing that is not quenched by any means.

इत्येवं वदन्ति जनजल्पनिर्भया एकमताः
कुमारव्यासशुकशाण्डिल्यगर्गविष्णुकौण्डिन्यशेषोद्धवारुणिबलिहनुमद्वि
भीषणाद्यो भक्त्याचार्याः ॥ ८३

ityevaṃ vadanti janajalpanirbhayā ekamatāḥ
kumāravyāsaśukaśāṇḍilyagargaviṣṇukauṇḍinyaś
eṣoddhavāruṇibalihanumadvibhīṣaṇādayo
bhaktyācāryāḥ ॥ 83

इत्येवम् वदन्ति जन-जल्प-निर्भयाः एक–मताः कुमार-व्यास-शुक-
शाण्डिल्य-गर्ग-विष्णु-कौण्डिन्य-शेष–उद्धव-अरुणि-बलि-हनुमत्-
विभीषण-आदयः भक्ति-आचार्याः ॥ ८३

इत्येवम् ^{0} जन-जल्प-निर्भयाः $^{m1/3}$ एक–मताः $^{m1/3}$ कुमार-
व्यास-शुक-शाण्डिल्य-गर्ग-विष्णु-कौण्डिन्य-शेष–उद्धव-अरुणि-बलि-
हनुमत्-विभीषण-आदयः$^{m1/3}$ भक्ति-आचार्याः$^{m1/3}$ वदन्ति $^{लट्\ iii/3}$॥

(from the beginning, regarding the entire text spoken of till now)

Such is the common opinion of the Bhakti Masters. It is untarnished by any lay prattle of society. A few enlightened souls are named in this verse:

Theme 83 Testimony

83. 1) Kumara - Sanatkumara, 2) Ved Vyasa, 3) Shukdeva - Vyasa's son, 4) Shandilya Rishi, 5) Garga, 6) Lord Vishnu, 7) Kaundinya – Shandilya's son, 8) Sheshnag – who manifested as Laxman, Balram, Patanjali, etc. 9) Uddhava, 10) Aruni – Uddalaka, 11) Bali – demon king, 12) Hanuman, 13) Vibhishan – Ravana's brother.

In modern times, this is known as Testimony or support for one's idea or product. Such a mention lends credence and makes the idea acceptable to more number of people easily.

य इदं नारदप्रोक्तं शिवानुशासनं विश्वसिति श्रद्त्ते स भक्तिमान् भवति
स प्रेष्ठं लभते स प्रेष्ठं लभते ॥ ८४

ya idaṃ nāradaproktaṃ śivānuśāsanam viśvasiti
śraddhatte sa bhaktimān bhavati sa preṣṭham
labhate sa preṣṭham labhate ॥ 84

यः इदम् नारद-प्रोक्तम् शिव-अनुशासनम् विश्वसिति श्रद्त्ते सः
भक्तिमान् भवति सः प्रेष्ठम् लभते सः प्रेष्ठम् लभते ॥ ८४

यः $^{m1/1}$ इदम् $^{n2/1}$ शिव-अनुशासनम् $^{n2/1}$ नारद-प्रोक्तम् $^{क \, n1/1}$
विश्वसिति $^{लट् \, iii/1}$ श्रद्त्ते $^{लट् \, iii/1}$

सः $^{m1/1}$ भक्तिमान् $^{m1/1}$ भवति $^{लट् \, iii/1}$

सः $^{m1/1}$ प्रेष्ठम् $^{m2/1}$ लभते $^{लट् \, iii/1}$

सः $^{m1/1}$ प्रेष्ठम् $^{m2/1}$ लभते $^{लट् \, iii/1}$ ॥

Whosoever believes and receives with faith and
reverence this auspicious teaching taught by Narada;
he is a Bhakta, he attains grace, he gets love, the
highest source of happiness.

॥ इति ॥ iti

Theme 84 Blessing

84. One is looking for something. What is it?

A miracle. What miracle?

That of finding love.

That of being showered by grace.

END

Sanskrit Grammar

Sandhis separated word by word पदच्छेद (प०),
Verses in prose order अन्वय (अ०), and with विभक्ति
Cases have been listed.

Nouns

> **m** masculine, **f** feminine, **n** neuter; **V** vocative
> **1/1** = vibhakti case from 1 to 7/number 1 to 3

Indeclinables (uninflected nouns or verbs) **0**
In Sanskrit the **adverbs** are mostly uninflected.

Verbs

> **iii/1** = person i to iii / number 1 to 3
> **PPP** = Past Participle Passive
> **PPA** = Past Participle Active, **PrPA** = Present

Since Sanskrit is an inflectional language, the **spelling of
the same word** changes as per context or usage. Hence
words can be **placed anywhere** in a sentence, as in poetic
use, without change in meaning. The matrix shows how.

Verb inflections in Sanskrit – a sample chart

982 गम् गतौ – to go, also in the sense of attainment		
Present Tense Active voice लट् कर्त्तरि		
Person/no	singular	dual	plural

Person/no	singular	dual	plural
Third	गच्छति iii/1	गच्छतः iii/2	गच्छन्ति iii/3
Second	गच्छसि ii/1	गच्छथः ii/2	गच्छथ ii/3
First	गच्छामि i/1	गच्छावः i/2	गच्छामः i/3

Masculine stem, vowel अ ending		
(रू–आ–म्–अ) राम ^m Lord's name		

	singular [1]	dual [2]	plural [3]
1 Doer	रामः $^{1/1}$	रामौ $^{1/2}$	रामाः $^{1/3}$
2 Object	रामम् $^{2/1}$	रामौ $^{2/2}$	रामान् $^{2/3}$
3 by	रामेण $^{3/1}$	रामाभ्याम् $^{3/2}$	रामैः $^{3/3}$
4 for	रामाय $^{4/1}$	रामाभ्याम् $^{4/2}$	रामेभ्यः $^{4/3}$
5 from	रामात् $^{5/1}$	रामाभ्याम् $^{5/2}$	रामेभ्यः $^{5/3}$
6 of	रामस्य $^{6/1}$	रामयोः $^{6/2}$	रामाणाम् $^{6/3}$
7 in	रामे $^{7/1}$	रामयोः $^{7/2}$	रामेषु $^{7/3}$
Vocative	हे राम $^{V/1}$	हे रामौ $^{V/2}$	हे रामाः $^{V/3}$

Masculine stem, consonant त् ending		
मरुत् ^m Wind, Breeze, Air		

	singular [1]	dual [2]	plural [3]
1 Doer	मरुत् $^{1/1}$	मरुतौ $^{1/2}$	मरुतः $^{1/3}$
2 Object	मरुतम् $^{2/1}$	मरुतौ $^{2/2}$	मरुतः $^{2/3}$
3 by	मरुता $^{3/1}$	मरुद्भ्याम् $^{3/2}$	मरुद्भिः $^{3/3}$
4 for	मरुते $^{4/1}$	मरुद्भ्याम् $^{4/2}$	मरुद्भ्यः $^{4/3}$
5 from	मरुतः $^{5/1}$	मरुद्भ्याम् $^{5/2}$	मरुद्भ्यः $^{5/3}$
6 of	मरुतः $^{6/1}$	मरुतोः $^{6/2}$	मरुताम् $^{6/3}$
7 in	मरुति $^{7/1}$	मरुतोः $^{7/2}$	मरुत्सु $^{7/3}$
Vocative	हे मरुत् $^{V/1}$	हे मरुतौ $^{V/2}$	हे मरुतः $^{V/3}$

Moods and Tenses in Sanskrit

1	लट्	Present Tense
2	लङ्	Imperfect Past Tense – *now and back*
3	लिट्	Perfect Past Tense – *yesterday and back*
4	लुङ्	Aorist Past Tense – *distant past*
5	लुट्	First Future Tense – *tomorrow onwards*
6	लृट्	Second Future Tense – *now onwards*
7	लोट्	Imperative Mood – *request*
8	वि॰लि॰	Potential Mood – *order*
9	आ॰लि॰	Benedictive Mood – *blessing*
10	लृङ्	Conditional Mood – *if/then*

References

https://naradabhaktisutrasl.blogspot.com/2018/02/chapter-ix.html

https://www.ashtangayoga.info/philosophy/sanskrit-and-devanagari/transliteration/

http://spokensanskrit.org/

KLV Sastry & Anantarama Sastri – Sabda Manjari 1961–Reprint - 2013 – RS Vadhyar & Sons, Palghat

Swami Akhandananda Saraswati - नारदभक्तिदर्शन – 2nd – 1969 – Satya Sahitya Prakashan Trust, Bombay

Swami Prabhupada - Narada Bhakti Sutra – 2nd – 1991 - Bhaktivedanta Book Trust, Mumbai

Swami Tyagisananda - Narada Bhakti Sutra – 1st – 2009 – Sri Ramakrishna Math, Chennai

Sri Sri Ravi Shankar – Narada Bhakti Sutra – 1st – 2009 – Sri Sri Publications Trust, Bangalore

Pushpa Dikshit – शीघ्रबोधव्याकरणम् – 2nd – 2017 – Pratibha Prakashan, Delhi

Epilogue

Mirabai 1498 – 1546 CE, Rajasthan. Bhakti Saint

Mere To Giridhar Gopal - M. S. Subbulakshmi

https://www.youtube.com/watch?v=26JoBNcsPuw

Mere To Giridhar Gopal – Vani Jairam

https://www.youtube.com/watch?v=fMdvoMJG6h4

https://www.youtube.com/watch?v=FMtPn6-fjq0

मेरे तो गिरिधर गोपाल दूसरो न कोई।मेरे तो गिरिधर गोपाल दूसरो न कोई।

जाके सर मोर मुकुट मेरो पति सोई । मेरे तो गिरिधर गोपाल दूसरो न कोई॥

अँसुवन जल सींच सींच प्रेम बेल बोई ।

अब तो बेल फैल गई आनन्द फल होई । मेरे तो गिरिधर गोपाल ॥

तात मात भ्रात बंधु आपनो न कोई । तात मात भ्रात बंधु अपनो न कोई ।

छोड़ गई कुल की कान काह करि है कोई । मेरे तो गिरिधर गोपाल ॥

चुनरी के किये टूक ओढ़ लीन्ही लोई। चुनरी के किये टूक ओढ़ लीन्ही लोई।

मोती मूँगे उतार बनमाला पोई । मेरे तो गिरिधर गोपाल दूसरो न कोई ॥२

जाके सर मोर मुकुट मेरो पति सोई।मेरे तो गिरिधर गोपाल दूसरो न कोई॥२

Man Tarpat Hari Darshan Ko Aaj - Mohammed Rafi

https://www.youtube.com/watch?v=XJCqDLLdKHY

Tora Mann Darpan Kehlaye – Asha Bhosle

https://www.youtube.com/watch?v=c44Ah24hr9M

सर्वे भवन्तु सुखिनः । सर्वे सन्तु निरामयाः ।

सर्वे भद्राणि पश्यन्तु । मा कश्चिद् दुःख भाग् भवेत् ॥

ॐ शान्तिः शान्तिः शान्तिः ॥

When faith has blossomed in life, Every step is led by the Divine. **Sri Sri Ravi Shankar**